Discipleship Inside Out™

NavPress is the publishing ministry of The Navigators, an international
Christian organization and leader in personal spiritual development.
NavPress is committed to helping people grow spiritually and enjoy
lives of meaning and hope through personal and group resources that
are biblically rooted, culturally relevant, and highly practical.

For a free catalog go to www.NavPress.com or call 1.800.366.7788
in the United States or 1.800.839.4769 in Canada.

NOTHING TO LOSE

a generation for desperation

Scott Dawson & Joey Hill

TABLE OF CONTENTS

INTRODUCTION

It's been said that the most dangerous person in the room is the one who has nothing to lose. We have learned this the hard way in our country with school shootings and terrorist attacks. But does that mean "nothing to lose" is only reserved for those who mean to do evil? I don't think so. You show me a guy who says, "What have I got to lose?" and risks it all to go out on a date with the new girl at school, and I will show you a dangerous ladies man. You show me a young lady who risks it all to ask for more responsibility from her boss, and I will show you a person who is dangerously closer to being someone else's boss. You show me a follower of Christ who has nothing to lose and I will show you a student on the devil's most dangerous list.

But what does that mean for someone who has everything to lose, like family, friends, or future plans? If someone is not dangerous, then what are they? Well, the opposite of dangerous is simply "safe." You show me something that is safe and I will show something that is locked up. That's the defining characteristic of a vault – typically called a safe – locked up.

Would you consider your life safe and locked up or dangerously risky? For those who play it safe, let me ask you if you have ever felt as if your life was living without you? As if the real you is buried behind your eyes and skin and it has no way out? Have you ever felt like the real you was losing the fight to these voices that dominate your thoughts? Have you ever screamed "No!" deep inside but yet gone ahead and done something anyway? Deep inside you want to change, but the days turn into months and years without one single thing in your life trans-formed. Do you feel like you keep covering the same ground in your life, but nothing ever shifts or is gained?

If you say yes to any of this, then let me be the bearer of bad news and good news. If you feel like you are no longer shifting the gears in your life it is simply because someone or something else is forcing you to ride shotgun while it runs your life for you. This is why you find yourself often saying things such as, "What was I thinking? Why did I do that? Who was that person last night? Does anyone know who I am?" While you may not want to hear something this heavy this early in a book, all of us have to understand one simple fact about how we were designed by the Great Designer. We were made to worship. It's as simple as that. Worship is in our DNA. Every fiber of your being wants to bow down to something, to put your hope in something, or to place all of your trust in something. Whether our families, our country, our dreams, our fame, our reputations, our passions, or even our worst critics, we naturally allow these things to dominate our thoughts and ultimately our actions. In essence we bow down. They become our little "g" gods of this age. They trap the real you inside and force the rest of your life to live according to script this world has laid out for you.

Ask yourself, "Have I ever been more emotional about something that happened to my life than about something that happened to Jesus' life?" Have I ever gotten more upset about someone attacking me than someone spreading false rumors about God? Does the uncertainty about my future on this planet scare me more than standing in front of God in judgment one day? If so, then your life is being smothered by the little "g gods" of this age and there is a high chance that you feel like a prisoner in your own life. Strange how similar a vault and a cell are when they're all locked up.

But what if I told you there is a get out of jail card with your name on it? This is the good news I was talking about earlier. There is a way to push back from the table of excess and selfishness to make room for something truly satisfying. You can get out of the trap that felt so safe at first. You can know real worship, real living, a real future, and real relationships. If you are ready to stop holding on to the sticky things of this world and start letting go, then take the 30-day challenge in the pages of this book. The first half of the book is devoted to things we tend to hold on to in life and how these can become weights that so easily hold us back. The second half is what happens when we let go. "Letting go is letting God" have His way in our lives.

This book is a countdown to freedom. You will actually start with Day 30 and work your way backwards to Day Zero. On Day Zero we will celebrate a life that has **Nothing to Lose**. So enjoy the ride and start your journey to freedom.

Scott Dawson

HOLDING
ON
TO YOUR PAST

"Therefore, if anyone is in Christ, he is a new creation. The old has passed away; behold, the new has come." **2 Corinthians 5:17**

HOLDING ON TO YOUR PAST

Did you know that the largest diamond in the world is 545.67 carats? It is named the Golden Jubilee diamond and is owned by the King of Thailand. The United States has the Hope Diamond in the Smithsonian Institute in Washington D.C., but it is only 45.52 carats. Diamonds are awesome and expensive, but they didn't start out that way. Remember from science class that all it takes to make a diamond is lots of pressure, lots of heat, and lots of time in the deep, dark earth below. After a few billion years they are mined, but they look nothing like the bling you might see on J. Lo's hand. They are ugly and rough. That is when a diamond cutter (yes, that is a real job) spends a lot of time turning the diamond into something beautiful and amazing. Pretty cool, huh?

Now, read 2 Corinthians 5:17. Paul, the guy who wrote 2 Corinthians, started the Corinthian church. You would think that since Paul started the church that everyone would love him, right? NOPE! Some people came into the church after Paul left and told the Corinthians that Paul wasn't good enough and shouldn't be trusted to lead the church. These "apostles", as they called themselves, pointed out how awesome they were and how dumb Paul was. Apparently one of the ways they tried to discredit Paul was by saying his past was too awful. According to these leaders, Paul was too dirty, too rough, and too bad to be loved by God. However, Paul reminds the Corinthian Christians that his and our worth is not found in the past, but in the future with Christ. Paul's past may have looked dark, but after encountering Jesus, he is a new creation.

The difference in our lives before and after experiencing Christ is just like the difference between the uncut and the cut diamond. The diamond goes from being a rock in the earth to being beautiful and expensive. If you saw the worlds biggest diamond before it was cut you probably would not be impressed. The diamond drastically changes when it is being cut. The old, ugly parts have to be cut away so that the beauty can be revealed.

We too are formed under a lot of pressure, heat, and darkness. When Christ found us we were ugly, unpolished, and stuck in some hard sins that we thought we wouldn't be able to quit. In fact, sometimes we have been living with those sins so long we're holding on simply because we are too afraid to let them go. We might even think it is too hard to change and we are just too comfortable where we are.

Are there things in your past that you are so ashamed of that you believe that God can't use you and maybe can't even love you? You are like an uncut diamond. Only a skilled master can turn you into a new creation that is valuable and useful. That skilled master is God! Christ has found you and mined you out of the dark, despairing earth. You are now in the light, but that doesn't mean you don't have any challenges. Now, for the first time you can clearly see all the darkness from your past. Don't crawl back into the hole! Quit holding on to the things that made you the way you used to be. God is going to shape you into a valuable new creation.

THINK ABOUT IT

What is one thing in your life you don't want anyone to know about because you are so ashamed?

PRAY ABOUT IT

Spend time asking God to cut away all the unwanted stuff that keeps you from being a new creation.

DO SOMETHING ABOUT IT

Go and don't be ashamed. When you feel guilty about your past, remind yourself that God is dealing with that and you don't have to feel guilty anymore. It is in your past. Your future lies with Christ as a new creation.

HOLDING ON
TO YOUR PAIN

"Come to me, all you who are weary and burdened, and I will give you rest." **Matthew 11:28**

HOLDING ON TO YOUR PAIN

Iron Man. He's probably the most popular super hero on the planet right now, thanks to Robert Downey Jr.'s portrayal in the box office hits Iron Man, Iron Man 2, and The Avengers – the film that broke box office records by making $200 million in its opening weekend. You probably know Iron Man's backstory by now, but here's a quick recap. A wealthy weapons engineer named Tony Stark is injured in an explosion while being kidnapped. Shrapnel from the explosion is lodged in his chest and, in order to save his life, a device is created that is inserted into his chest to keep the metal fragments from his heart. While in captivity Stark develops a weaponized flying suit in order to escape his kidnappers. Iron Man is born and the rest, as they say, is history.

Similar to the device in Tony Stark's chest that protects his heart and gives him a second chance at life, Jesus has made an offer to intercede on our behalf. He wants to give rest to our tired hearts. In Matthew 11:28, while speaking to a crowd, Jesus says, "Come to me, all you who are weary and burdened, and I will give you rest." This verse makes some people feel warm and fuzzy inside. For others, however, it might seem like "rest" is a luxury that is too far out of reach.

Consider Jesus' audience here. These are people who were spiritually fatigued. Most of their religious leaders, namely the Pharisees, spent their time ridiculing people because they weren't "good enough." So you can imagine that when Jesus invited those in the crowd to follow Him and enjoy the gift of His rest, there were some who may not have been convinced. Many of these people, like some of us today, had grown up being told that they had to perform a certain number of religious chores in order to enjoy God. There is no doubt that some of Jesus' audience had their fair share of junk floating around their hearts, a wide variety of pain that they were holding on to. And due to the pain of insecurity and fear living inside of them, it seems likely that they had to pause and think, is this too good to be true?

No person is immune to pain. Not even the super heroes in blockbuster movies. Everyone has broken pieces of their lives stored away somewhere inside of them and when we hold on to these things we are, in essence, allowing them to inch closer to our hearts. Maybe the broken pieces that we are holding on to represent a divorce, bullying, abuse, loss, or a series of mistakes. Whatever the case, the invitation and promise Jesus made to that crowd a couple thousand years ago extends to us because that very same Jesus is alive with us today.

Tony Stark's life depended on keeping the dangerous shrapnel from his heart. Similarly, our lives—or at least the lives God created us to live—require that we stop holding on to our pain and allow Christ to remove the shards from our hearts. It is not for us to hold on to the pain of life or attempt to cover it up. Christ offers us His rest in exchange for our weariness and burdens.

THINK ABOUT IT
What are some different kinds of pain that you are holding on to right now?

PRAY ABOUT IT
Once you have identified the pain in your life, take time to approach God in prayer, thanking Him for His promises and asking for His help.

DO SOMETHING ABOUT IT
If any of the pain you identified involves other people in your life, ask God to show how you can address this pain with them, and then go do it.

HOLDING ON

TO YOUR UNFORGIVENESS

"Therefore, as God's chosen people, holy and dearly loved, clothe yourselves with compassion, kindness, humility, gentleness and patience. Bear with each other and forgive whatever grievances you may have against one another. Forgive as the Lord forgave you." **Colossians 3:12-13**

At the fateful sentencing of Jerry Sandusky, the infamous man in the midst of a child abuse scandal that rocked Penn State and the entire nation, Victim No. 6 relayed the following message: "If you seek forgiveness, Jesus will forgive you. There's not any other way. Please repent, or there is a bigger judgment to come." Victim No. 4, however, had a different message: "I will not forgive you, Jerry Sandusky. I will not forgive you . . ."

Hurt can come from many places, and the closer someone is to us, the more pain he or she can cause. People who care about us aren't supposed to hurt us, right?! That's why church scandals, abuse by those we trust, divorce, and abandonment hurt. And that's why forgiveness is so difficult to offer when pain is real.

Without a doubt, Victim No. 6, Victim No. 4 and all of the other victims who experienced such tragic events in their childhood have had to endure countless affects of one man's sin. It is not an act that can be flippantly forgotten, and it should not be. It would be irresponsible to forget; acknowledging it serves as a warning to all of us and as justice to his victims. But Victim No. 6 knows that healing is truly available, and that it is available only through the forgiving power of Christ.

Read Colossians 3:12-13. Paul wanted believers to fully understand that we are sinners who have completely betrayed Christ with our sin. Christ took the complete punishment for our sins, and because of that He can forgive us, and we stand in perfect righteousness before God. Our forgiveness came at great cost to Him and had nothing to do with our own worthiness. Paul clearly stated that we had betrayed Christ, and He forgave us anyway. We did nothing to earn His forgiveness. In fact, there's nothing we could ever do to earn it. Nothing. And yet, He forgave anyway. It is this amazing and undeserved forgiveness that Paul said drives believers to offer forgiveness to others.

When others hurt us, our first reaction is often to get revenge or to cut them off from our lives. But Scripture tells us that we are to offer the same forgiveness to others as Christ offered us. It's OK if we think they don't deserve it. Just like Paul described, forgiveness is not based on the worth of the offending party but the power of Christ in the one who forgives. When we forgive others we are relinquishing our right to get back at them; we are relinquishing bitterness that we harbor in our hearts; we are relinquishing the chains by which anger and bitterness enslave us. When we forgive, we are showing our offenders the gospel of forgiveness in Jesus Christ, the only One who can eternally forgive.

THINK ABOUT IT

Who have you denied forgiveness because of your own sinful desires for revenge? How has holding onto your anger and bitterness hurt you?

PRAY ABOUT IT

Ask God to reveal the sinfulness in your own heart and to give you the power to forgive.

DO SOMETHING ABOUT IT

If possible, contact those who have hurt you and ask their forgiveness for your bitterness toward them, explain your pain, and then express your forgiveness toward them. If contacting a person directly is not possible, write them a letter, even if they will never read it.

HOLDING ON

TO YOUR PARENTS' DREAMS

"'For I know the plans I have for you,' declares the Lord, 'plans to prosper you and not to harm you, plans to give you hope and a future.'" **Jeremiah 29:11**

HOLDING ON TO YOUR PARENTS' DREAMS

Vanessa and Bethany grew up in a homeschool family that defined "homeschool" as teaching girls how to change diapers and wash dishes in order to someday be a good housewife. Neither of them took a written test until their GED. Today they're struggling to peel back the onion layers just to discover who they are and what God has made them to be.

Nate knew while he was still in middle school that God wanted to do something great with his life. But when he talked to his parents about it they convinced him there was no need to "go overboard" with his faith. Now he's a senior in high school, applying to local colleges, even though he has no idea what to major in.

Most parents want what's best for their child. And that's great but what happens when that child is 18 and about to graduate high school? What happens when Dad says: "I didn't work 50 hours a week and send you to a good school for you to spend your life working in some orphanage in Africa!" or when Mom says: "Honey, I'm all for reading the Bible, but don't make major life decisions based on it."? What happens when your parents' plan for your life gets in the way of God's plan for your life? Jeremiah 29:11 says, "'For I know the plans I have for you' declares the Lord, 'plans to prosper you and not to harm you, plans to give you hope and a future.'" There it is. God has a plan for you. He already knows what it is. And it's good.

God gave those words to Jeremiah to speak to the Israelites while they were living as captives in Babylon. They were exiles, political hostages. Someone else had chosen their future and their future was hopeless. Half of Israel had been destroyed and dispersed to the corners of the world by the Assyrians. Some time later, the rest were taken as prisoners to Babylon. Years passed. Hope vanished. Into that situation, God gave a word of hope. In verse 14, God says, "[I] will bring you back from captivity." No matter what your situation or what your parents' plans for you might be, God has a plan for you.

HOLDING ON TO YOUR PARENTS' DREAMS

Some of you are very familiar with the chasm between what your parents' dreams for your life are and what you think God's plans are. Some of you might have to think about it a while. Some of your parents might not have dreams for your life. Be bold in taking up your cross and following Jesus even when it looks to the world and to your parents like you hate them.

THINK ABOUT IT

Think about your relationship with your parents. What do you think your parents' dreams for your life are? What do you think God's plans for your life might be?

PRAY ABOUT IT

Ask God to give you clear direction for your life.

DO SOMETHING ABOUT IT

Sometime in the next 24 hours talk with your parents about what they want for your life and, if you have an idea, what you think God's plans are for your life.

HOLDING ON

TO YOUR DREAMS

"Jesus looked at him and loved him. 'One thing you lack,' he said. 'Go, sell everything you have and give to the poor, and you will have treasure in heaven. Then come, follow me.'" **Mark 10:21**

HOLDING ON TO YOUR DREAMS

Have you ever heard of Habitat for Humanity? It is an organization that builds homes for people who can't afford houses. In fact, Habitat has built over 500,000 houses and housed over 2.5 million people! Pretty awesome, huh? And it all started with one guy who had a dream.

Millard Fuller (that's the guy's name) was like a lot of people who had a dream to be rich. At the age of six, his first business was raising and selling pigs for his daddy while living in Lanett, Alabama. Growing up he sold rabbits, cows, even mistletoe. He worked hard and saved his money. He received an economics degree from Auburn University and a law degree from the University of Alabama. Then he and a friend of his went into business and by the time he was 29 years old he was a millionaire. That is pretty cool, right? Lets look at another rich man.

Read Mark 10:17-22. This rich guy had apparently achieved his dreams of riches, too. He must have had the nicest clothes, thrown the coolest parties, and even been a pretty good religious guy, yet he must have felt something missing in his life when he went looking for Jesus. Notice at the end of verse 21 Jesus says the same thing to this rich guy that He said to His disciples – "Follow me." But the rich guy didn't. He held on to his dreams of riches. What would it have been like if he said 'yes'?

Well, Millard Fuller did say 'yes'. After earning all that money, Millard Fuller wasn't happy and he found himself almost losing his family. So he and his wife accepted the call to follow Christ and decided to give all their riches away. They sold their nice cars, big house, and their successful business. They didn't hold on to any of it. A few years later God gave the Fullers a new dream, to build affordable houses for the poor as a way to share the Gospel.

What are your dreams? You know, dreams are not bad. Even dreams of having lots of money are not a bad thing. The question is: Do you value those dreams over Christ? Would you give up your dreams and follow Christ? You may honestly say 'no'. Pray God gives you the strength to give up any dreams that are distracting you from Him. That is what

Jesus asked the rich young man to do. His dreams of wealth, power, and social status were in the way of what his soul longed to have – eternal life that can only be found in the Savior, Jesus Christ.

When the rich guy from the parable said 'no' to following Jesus he went away sad and confused. The needs of his soul and the dreams he had for himself were two different things. He went away unsatisfied. However, when Millard Fuller said 'yes' he went away satisfied and God gave him a new dream that led him to serve people all over the world. Don't hold on to your dreams. Give them to God and follow Him.

THINK ABOUT IT

What are you dreaming about and pursuing that you would not give up to know Christ more?

PRAY ABOUT IT

Can you think of a dream that you wouldn't give up to follow Jesus? If so, pray today for God to change what you value. Or ask God to show you what you are putting above Him.

DO SOMETHING ABOUT IT

Write down your to do list for today. How much time are you spending pursuing your dream? Make time in your schedule to pursue God.

HOLDING ON

TO YOUR REPUTATION

"Am I now trying to win the approval of men, or of God? Or am I trying to please men? If I were still trying to please men, I would not be a servant of Christ." **Galatians 1:10**

Facebook now has 1 billion active users each month. That is 1/6 of the world's population. Chances are you are among the 1 billion, and when you signed up for Facebook and created an account you were given your own page. This page represents your own personal "real estate" on the site where you can post pictures from your life and share your thoughts and interests.

Since the Facebook craze began, people have been carefully crafting their online images. Whenever someone posts a picture from the cool birthday party they were at or presses the "like" button for a band's fan page, they are shaping their social networking reputation. But it is not enough to simply post a picture or status update. Many users check their Facebook account religiously to see if anyone has "liked" or commented on their postings.

Almost 2000 years ago, the Apostle Paul had a habit of praising churches in the opening verses of his letters to them. You might call this Paul's version of a "like" button. However, that was not the case with his letter to the Christians in Galatia. Instead, Paul immediately confronted the Galatian church because they had accepted a false gospel brought to them by false teachers who likely wanted little more than popular appeal.

Open your Bible and read Galatians 1:10. Paul wrote, "Am I now trying to win the approval of men, or of God? Or am I trying to please men? If I were still trying to please men, I would not be a servant of Christ." Paul's point is pretty clear: he is more concerned with his reputation before God than he is with his reputation before the recipients of his letter. If the approval of people was more important to Paul than the approval of God, then he would have simply told them whatever they wanted to hear, and he would have been no different from the false teachers giving people a false gospel.

Of course, there is nothing inherently wrong with having a Facebook account. Social networking can be a great way to stay in touch with friends and family. However, if we find ourselves doing activities just so we can tell everyone online that we are doing them or if we obsessively document our lives on social networking sites, then it would appear that we are overly concerned with our reputations. This is not to say that we should not be mindful of our reputations. As some people have learned the hard way, once you create a certain reputation it can be very difficult to undo.

Trying to "clean up" your online image can prove difficult, especially if there are photos of you and comments you made in the past floating around on other people's pages. But if we are consumed with concern for our reputation in this world, then how much focus can we really be giving to our relationship with Christ? When we hold too tightly to our reputation among people, regardless of whether it is a good reputation or a bad one, we are limiting the attention that we can give to our reputation before God.

THINK ABOUT IT

In what ways does your concern for your reputation affect your relationship with God?

PRAY ABOUT IT

Pray and ask God to give you the courage we see in Paul, the courage to place our reputation with God above our public image.

DO SOMETHING ABOUT IT

Take a moment to identify the different ways you try to define and hold on to your reputation, whether that is through Facebook, sports, relationships, or other things, and write those down.

HOLDING ON

TO YOUR FAME

"'Not so with you. Instead, whoever wants to become great among you must be your servant, and whoever wants to be first must be slave of all. For even the Son of Man did not come to be served, but to serve, and to give his life as a ransom for many.'" **Mark 10:43-45**

HOLDING ON TO YOUR FAME

Imagine a list of the people in your class or social circle in order of their popularity. The most popular people are at the top of the list and the least popular are at the bottom. Visualize this list of names, each representing a person and his or her popularity compared to others. Now imagine that each name in this list from top to bottom of the social order is a rung in a ladder.

You and I both know that if everyone in your class were on a ladder of popularity, nearly all of them would be trying to climb to the top. That means people really only want to socialize with people higher than themselves on the ladder in order to move up. Boys only want to date girls up the ladder. Girls only want to date boys up the ladder. Friends only want friends up the ladder. Because if you hang out with people further down the popularity ladder than yourself, they'll drag you down. And if you have to knock a few people down in order to move up, just consider it collateral damage.

There's just one problem with this scenario: it's exactly the opposite of what Jesus modeled and taught. Read Mark 10:35-45. Here, two of Jesus' followers, James and John, asked Jesus for the two most important positions in His kingdom. They were jockeying for position. In Matthew's account of the same story, it's the mother of James and John who asked Jesus on behalf of her sons. Their popularity was so important to her.

When the rest of the disciples found out, they felt stepped over, kicked down the ladder. Jesus corrected them all. He basically said, "I know this is how everyone else acts, pushing each other down in order to make it to the top. But that's not how you should act. If you want to find your way to the top of my ladder, work your way down to the bottom."

In the end, Jesus is going to flip the ladder. If you're holding on to your own fame, your own place on the ladder, you're in for a rude awakening. What you're looking for is not at the top. Don't waste your life climbing up the ladder looking for what can only be found at the bottom. Stop. Jump off the ladder. And find true happiness in the outstretched arms of your Savior at the bottom.

THINK ABOUT IT

Think about how you treat the people in your school and youth group. Do you treat those you consider up the ladder from yourself differently than those down the ladder? Do you give full attention to those above you, laughing at their jokes (even when they aren't funny) and listening to their stories (even when they aren't interesting)? Do you belittle those below you, ignoring them and putting them down?

PRAY ABOUT IT

Pray that God would help you to see your own fame how He sees it. And ask God to begin showing you how to begin moving down the ladder.

DO SOMETHING ABOUT IT

Make a conscious effort to serve others, especially those beneath you. Listen to them. Eat lunch at their table. Defend them against bullies. Make your way to the bottom of the ladder.

HOLDING ON
TO THE NOISE

"The world and its desires pass away, but the man who does the will of God lives forever."
1 John 2:17

HOLDING ON TO THE NOISE

READ THIS! LOOK AT ME! BUY THIS! CLICK HERE! DOWNLOAD NOW! WATCH THIS! FREE! FREE! FREE! OMG! BOGO! ROFL!

BILLBOARDS! INTERNET ADS! MAGAZINE RACKS! TXT MSGS! SOCIAL MEDIA! TV! PHONE! MUSIC!

BOYFRIEND! GIRLFRIEND! BEST FRIEND! PARENT! TEACHER! COACH!

Do you ever just want to go into your room, shut the door and turn of the NOISE?!?

Do you ever feel like everyone and everything is telling you what music to like, what food to eat, what clothes to wear, where to go, what to do and who to be? Sometimes it seems impossible to hear God through all the NOISE.

We read in 1 John 2:17 that, "The world and its desires pass away, but the man who does the will of God lives forever."

Many teens wake to music from their phone, check Facebook, Twitter, Instagram, text messages, etc, get dressed with the TV on, drive to school while talking on the phone with the radio on… math class, pop quiz, lunchroom, practice, homework – all the while texting and checking social media.

The problem is that none of those things last. All the things the world is trying to sell you, the things you should buy and the things you should be, are temporary. Tomorrow they'll be gone. A life spent chasing after the desires of the world is a life wasted. It's like buying stock in a bankrupt company or betting on a football team without a quarterback. It's a sure loss.

The sad thing is that the world does a great job selling stuff we don't need and most of the time people take the bait. We don't know how to

HOLDING ON TO THE NOISE

be content. We don't know how to slow down long enough or be still and quiet long enough to debrief and process life with God in prayer.

Do you ever wonder why you never hear God? How long is the lengthiest time you went in quiet, with no advertisements, no noise, just you and God? For starters, the rest of this page will be blank… take a minute to recognize all the NOISE surrounding you, holding on to your attention instead of allowing you to give it fully to God.

THINK ABOUT IT

Think about your daily routine. Is there time built in to reflect and pray? Perhaps this time right now is it. What might you need to cut out of your daily schedule in order to cut out the noise?

PRAY ABOUT IT

Pray that God would show you creative ways to find quiet. Perhaps more importantly, pray that God would do something awesome, maybe even speak to you, during that quiet time.

DO SOMETHING ABOUT IT

Turn things off at night: your phone, television, music, computer. One day a week, leave your phone at home, leave the radio off in the car, unplug your television, disconnect your internet service. Make time and space to hear God!

HOLDING ON

TO THE CRITICS

"But God chose the foolish things of the world to shame the wise; God chose the weak things of the world to shame the strong." **1 Corinthians 1:27**

HOLDING ON TO THE CRITICS

Everyone has been hit by harsh criticism. Elvis Presley, the King of Rock and Roll, was told at a young age that he couldn't sing. Thomas Edison, the inventor of the light bulb, had a grade school teacher that told him he was stupid. Twenty-seven different publishers turned down Dr. Seuss' book. A newspaper fired Walt Disney for not having enough imagination. Each of these critics thought of these men as fools with foolish ideas.

The truth is, we all have harsh critics in our lives. You know its funny what sticks in our minds. We could get a thousand compliments in one day and all we remember is the one harsh criticism. That old saying of, "I'm rubber, you're glue, whatever you say bounces off of me and sticks to you," is just not true most of the time. Those hateful words make us feel stupid and foolish. How you ever thought about how God thinks of you?

Read 1 Corinthians 1:18-2:5. Apparently, Paul was a little unpolished. He didn't speak as well as others. He often came into town dirty or beaten up from being persecuted or put in jail somewhere else. Other leaders had come into Corinth, impressing the people and being cooler or more interesting than Paul. Some people began to compare and criticize Paul, turning church into a popularity contest; but Paul changed their opinions by pointing to the cross of Jesus.

By the world's standard, Jesus dying on the cross was kind of foolish. Here is Jesus, God as a human, betrayed and publicly humiliated as he is executed. Why didn't Jesus use his power so He wouldn't be killed? Remember even the guy on a cross next to Him said, "Aren't you the Christ? Save yourself and us!" (Luke 23:39) Paul reminds the Corinthians that even though Jesus' death looked foolish, it was a part of God's perfect plan. Because Jesus died on the cross, He took the punishment for our sin, and we are able to have a relationship with God. Paul then argued that while the world thought Jesus' sacrifice was foolish, God knew it was wise. In the same way, even though the world thinks that we are foolish, God can actually use us to show His awesomeness.

HOLDING ON TO THE CRITICS

God can use any willing heart to do great things, even one the world looks down upon. D.L. Moody was an evangelist in the 1800s. His dad died when he was 4. He grew up very poor, and only had a 3rd grade education, but God used him to share Christ with millions of people, to start a church, to found three schools, and start a publishing company. Brother Lawrence was a French monk who lived in the 1600s. He worked in the monastery kitchen all his life (over 50 years) and tried to always live in God's presence. After he died, a student of his published Brother Lawrence's letters as a book called *The Practice of the Presence of God* that has lead millions of people to a deeper relationship with God.

God uses ordinary people, who the world may think are foolish, to love and show love to others. Do you think sometimes that God can't use you because you're too shy, plain, or dumb? Don't hold on to those criticisms! Jesus was mocked and you will be too, but Jesus knew what his Father thought of him. Do you know how your Heavenly Father thinks of you? He created you and is pleased with you. Isn't it time for you to see yourself the way God sees you?

THINK ABOUT IT
What are some harsh criticisms that you are holding on to as truth?

PRAY ABOUT IT
Ask God to help you see yourself through His eyes instead of listening to critics.

DO SOMETHING ABOUT IT
When someone makes fun of you, remind yourself that they don't see you as God sees you.

HOLDING ON

TO CONVENIENCE

"There is a way that seems right to a man, but in the end it leads to death." **Proverbs 14:12**

Modern society, at least here in the United States, seems fixated on convenience. Some of the greatest examples of this are found in the slew of products that have been released in the past several years. Take, for instance, Smucker's release of "Goober PB & J," which combines peanut butter and jelly in a single jar for those who do not have the time or energy to open two different containers. But our fixation with convenience is also evident in the things we say.

When Sean was a sophomore in college he worked as a lifeguard at a neighborhood pool. One sunny Sunday afternoon, as Sean was sitting in his lifeguard chair, he overheard an older man seated next to him having a heated conversation. The man was loud and clearly upset. As Sean listened he soon realized that the man was talking about his church. Apparently, the man's church had recently altered its service times and this change in schedule conflicted with the man's Sunday nap. "It is a thorn in my side," exclaimed the man.

It is plain to see that convenience has become more and more of a priority in recent decades, even within the church. Like the older gentleman at the pool, we consider any obstacles to our convenience as thorns in our sides. In many people's minds it seems only right and fair that life be as easy and trouble-free as possible. But we cannot always trust our instincts, especially when it comes to our feelings about convenience.

Open your Bible and read Proverbs 14:12. Solomon, one of the wisest men to ever live, wrote, "There is a way that seems right to a man, but in the end it leads to death." Clearly, things that are convenient are not necessarily deadly, but they still lead to death. Think about it. Is Smucker's "Goober PB & J" convenient? Yes—whether it tastes good is another question entirely. Is Smucker's "Goober PB & J" going to prevent you from dying someday? Not likely. Therefore, it leads to death, just like a host of other products that are convenient but useless to save us.

HOLDING ON TO CONVENIENCE

Solomon was on to something when he said that certain things seem "right" to us but they end in death. In the twenty-first century convenience seems "right." However, a convenience-focused mindset will not lead to eternal life. A convenience-focused mindset teaches us to look for the fast and easy way, for the path of least resistance, for the shortcuts to success; but a life bent on convenience will not lead to abundant life. Conveniences are the things we are willing to purchase, like Smucker's "Goober PB & J." Inconveniences are the things we are willing to complain about, like the old man by the pool grieving his lost naptime. But they are not so important that we are willing to die for them, fight for them, or devote our lives to them. That being the case, we should stop holding so forcefully to convenience.

There is nothing inherently wrong with enjoying the perks of convenience, but when we hold on to convenience like a drowning man gripping on to a lifejacket, there is a problem because this stuff does not save us.

THINK ABOUT IT
What are some ways you may have been treating your faith in Jesus like a convenience rather than a conviction?

PRAY ABOUT IT
Pray and ask God for a change of heart, for the willingness to place the things that lead to life above the conveniences that do not.

DO SOMETHING ABOUT IT
What are some conveniences that you are holding too firmly to and what steps will you take to place Christ above all else?

HOLDING

ON

TO SELFISHNESS

"Your attitude should be the same as that of Christ Jesus." **Philippians 2:5**

HOLDING ON TO SELFISHNESS

One of the most poignant images from the historic day of September 11, 2001 is that of firefighters running up the stairs, toward a fiery inferno inside a World Trade Tower as thousands of people were evacuating and running down the stairs. And it is these images that give numerous children aspirations of becoming firemen—their lives are ones of sacrifice and selflessness for the good of others. These are the traits of heroes: selflessness and sacrifice.

Selflessness is the trait of a hero. We even give awards and medals to people who display selflessness and sacrifice in the face of danger. People love a good hero story. So, why do so few of us act like heroes? Our sinful human nature is not predisposed to thinking about others. We are consumed with believing that we are the center of our own personal universes.

Read Philippians 2:3-8. Paul told his readers in verse 5 that they should have the same attitude that Jesus did. He described what this attitude looked like in verses 3 and 4. Paul instructed believers to mirror the kind of humility that Jesus demonstrated when He obediently gave up all of the privileges of the righteous King of the universe to take on the form of a man, and to become a servant to men at that. Jesus came with the attitude of service. Even as the King of Kings, He would be obedient to die a sacrificial death on behalf of those who did not deserve it. It was to this mindset of selfless humility that Paul called believers. The universe does belong to God, and He alone is at the center of it. And yet, Christ demonstrated a continual attitude of selflessness during His life on earth.

Paul did not mean that believers are never to care for themselves. But Paul was speaking of an overarching attitude that accompanies us in life. This world is not about us, and we must not act as if it is. If we are to imitate Christ, then we must not seek to benefit ourselves at the expense of others. Rather, we are to consider the interests of others as much as we consider our own. We do not live in isolation, and we cannot act as if others are here for our benefit. As we become more like Christ we display His character and gospel as we embody the selfless and sacrificial traits of our Savior.

THINK ABOUT IT

How is selfishness the root of almost all sin against others, including God?

PRAY ABOUT IT

Thank God for His selfless acts toward you and ask Him to show you how you have been selfish.

DO SOMETHING ABOUT IT

Who have you been hurting or disrespecting by seeking to benefit at his or her expense? Ask for that person's forgiveness this week.

HOLDING ON TO WHAT IF

"Humble yourselves, therefore, under God's mighty hand, that he may lift you up in due time. Cast all your anxiety on him because he cares for you." **1 Peter 5:6-7**

HOLDING ON TO WHAT IF

There have been a number of "Worst-Case Scenario" items that seek to educate the human population on what to do if you find yourself in a worst-case scenario, such as dangling precariously off the side of a cliff in your car. Television shows have re-launched, books have been published, and even a board game is available. These are not just novelty items nor are they useless pieces of information in case you ever have a "Worst-Case Scenario" category on a game show. For those who live in fear of the "What Ifs", this kind of knowledge is necessary because, in their minds, the worst-case scenario is always around the corner. Continually fearing the unknown is paralyzing and causes much anguish.

There may be good reasons why you live in fear. Life circumstances like an unexpected death in the family, tragedies in the community, hurricanes, tornadoes, or health issues may have taught you that suffering is all too real and, although God is in control, bad things can still happen to His children. Frankly, that can be a scary truth to realize. It leaves you wondering what bad things could happen in the future. It leaves you wondering what worst-case scenario will happen at any moment. But allowing such fear to paralyze your joy is a tragedy and is ultimately rooted in what you believe about God and what you believe about yourself.

Read 1 Peter 5:6-7. Did you notice the last few words of that passage? Read it again. God cares for you. It's right there. In the Bible. God cares for you. You may be able to articulate in perfect theological words that God loves His people, but a lack of belief in His care for you personally will cripple your trust in His good, wise, and sovereign character. You may believe that God is sovereign, but if you don't believe He cares for you, then you are simply waiting for Him to plan what painful struggles He will throw your way next. But that's just not truth. Read it again. God cares for you. Peter told his audience that they can trust Him and unload all of their worries, anxieties, and what ifs onto the Lord, because He cares for them. And, He not only cares for them, but we know that He is sovereign over our lives. He has the will and the ability to take care of us and to be present with us when He sovereignly allows pain into our lives.

Notice, though, that Peter begins these verses with the command to be humble before the mighty God. This command carries two meanings. The first is that we must submit to God's authority in our lives. Whatever is happening to us or around us is under His wise control. Nothing happens outside of His control, and we must humbly remember that we are not God. The second meaning is that we humbly give our worries to Him. We do it humbly because worrying is ultimately an issue of pride; worrying indicates that we are taking on all of our concerns instead of entrusting them to our caring and mighty God.

Trusting and believing that God cares for you is essential to releasing the fear of the "What Ifs". God is not enjoying watching you suffer; neither does He find joy in your pain. He cares about you. Equally essential is viewing God for who He is and us for who we are. He is sovereign, wise, and good. We are not Him and we must humbly entrust our lives to His care and wise control. When we are able to do this, we will feel the enslavement of paralyzing fear lose its grip on us.

THINK ABOUT IT

What things in life do you fear the most? What do you fear the most about God?

PRAY ABOUT IT

Praise God for His sovereign wisdom and control, for His goodness, and for His love and care for you. Ask Him to help your unbelief in those areas.

DO SOMETHING ABOUT IT

Make a list of all of the "What Ifs" or fears that prevent you from living abundantly in Christ. Then, near each list item, write why you can entrust that to God.

HOLDING ON
TO WHAT'S FAIR

"Therefore, since we have been justified through faith, we have peace with God through our Lord Jesus Christ, through whom we have gained access by faith into this grace in which we now stand. And we rejoice in the hope of the glory of God." **Romans 5:1-2**

HOLDING ON TO WHAT'S FAIR

Daniel loved to play football. He started playing when he was 4 in a recreational league and wanted to play for a big school in college. Even though he was short for a running back He started on the varsity high school team when he was a sophomore. By his senior year he was second in the state in rushing yards with over 1500 yards for the regular season. The local news channel loved to interview him and show clips of his big plays, but when the colleges started recruiting, nobody came knocking on his door. Colleges came and talked to other players on his team that did not work as hard as he did, nor have the stats he had. When he asked the college recruiters why they weren't talking to him they said, "You're just a little too short." "It's not fair," he said, "it's just not fair."

We like things to be fair. If your mom gives your sister $20 then you should get $20, right? That is only fair, but when we start walking with Christ the idea of fairness changes.

Read Romans 5:1-2. These two verses are anything but fair. Just as when we disobey our parents and get punished, so also when we disobey God a punishment is required. That punishment is death, but as you can see, though we have sinned, we are not dead. Paul tells us "we have been justified through faith." We have not been justified through our actions. Jesus Christ took the punishment for our sins and made everything right. That means we have been justified and we believe (or have faith) that Christ's sacrifice is enough and so we have been "justified through faith." What does this give us? It gives us peace, hope, and access to grace that allows us to have a deep, loving relationship with our Creator, God.

Think of it this way. Let's say you are a girl. (If you are, great! If you are a guy then just hold on. It makes the story less confusing.) You want to marry this guy you have been dating, but you can't because you smashed his parent's car 2 years ago and you have not paid them for the damages. You are afraid the parents hate you so you avoid them at all cost. It doesn't look like there will be wedding bells in your future. But wait! Your guy wants to marry you so much that he pays his parents for your damages so you can get married and have a loving relationship with his parents. That is the gospel! It is beautiful. It is wonderful. But, it isn't fair.

Therefore, since you have been treated unfairly you should not demand fairness around you. The simple fact of the matter is that life is unfair. You may have had an experience like Daniel in which you worked really hard at something but nothing came out of it. It would be easy to become bitter about that, but don't! You may want to retaliate or do something to get even with someone because you were not treated fairly, but God does not want you to do that. What does he want you to do? He wants you to remember the same unfair love, mercy, and grace He showed you. Quit holding on to what's fair and show the same unfair love that Christ first showed you.

THINK ABOUT IT

Can you think of some bitter feelings you are holding on to because you were treated unfairly?

PRAY ABOUT IT

Ask God to change your heart. Every time you feel bitter about being treated unfairly ask God to remove that bitterness.

DO SOMETHING ABOUT IT

Show some of God's unfair love today. Help someone you might feel doesn't deserve God's love – in fact, none of us did.

HOLDING ON

TO WORLDLY CONFIDENCE

"But whatever was to my profit I now consider loss for the sake of Christ." **Philippians 3:7**

HOLDING ON TO WORLDLY CONFIDENCE

Résumés can say a lot about a person. In fact, when applying for a job, résumés are essential for telling a potential employer about certain aspects of your experience, skills, extra-curricular activities, and more. They provide a chance to show off and "market" yourself to others. Some people, though, want to look better than their actual qualifications, so they lie on their résumés. Take, for instance, George O'Leary, who was forced to resign after just five days as head football coach of Notre Dame. Why such a short tenure? O'Leary claimed to have a Master's Degree from New York University and to have been a lettering football player in college. Both were lies, and O'Leary readily and apologetically admitted as much as he resigned.

Why would someone lie about accomplishments? It seems that humans are so driven to place confidence in accomplishments and achievements that we will make them up. Having more bullet points on our résumé falsely gives us great confidence in who we are and in what we can do. Some of us even try to work our way toward an impressive "spiritual" résumé. We either do this because it's what we think we should do as a "good" Christian or because we think that we can somehow earn God's approval with good behavior.

Many of the Jewish leaders had this same mindset. They prided themselves in their accomplishments and were confident that their legalistic behavior was earning favor with God. And then, when Christ came, some of these same Jews insisted that new believers had to first become Jews in order to fully follow Christ. Paul, however, had no confidence in what man can do.

Read Philippians 3:3-10. Paul could have ended verse 7 with "Boom!" The résumé he laid out gave a picture of the ideal Jew in every way. But, he stated that even he could not have confidence in his genealogy or achievements, his intellect or his service, his passion or his "good" behavior. Paul stated that his confidence wasn't in his own righteousness, no matter how admirable it appeared; rather, he said that his righteousness was found in that of God, which comes through faith.

His résumé could have been his idol. Instead, Christ was his only confidence. Everything else that he had been or achieved, Paul counted as trash compared to knowing Christ, his Lord.

Paul did not mean that living in Christ's righteousness is worthless. Displaying God's character by obeying His Word shows the fruit of righteousness in our lives. But that fruit is not what we place confidence in. Paul could have been the most confident Jew in the land, but he considered his life nothing without Christ. We can do all the right things, go through all the right motions, and give all the right answers, but we cannot put confidence in ourselves. The accomplishments we have in this world cannot earn us favor with God or secure salvation for us. Only the righteousness of Christ can change us and bring salvation and a heart that desires to obey Him.

THINK ABOUT IT

What about your life gives you confidence? How is that confidence becoming an idol?

PRAY ABOUT IT

Confess the way that you have been trying to earn righteousness or favor with God and thank God that because of His salvation, you can place your confidence solely in Him.

DO SOMETHING ABOUT IT

Evaluate the things you do that just keep you busy and have no eternal impact. How can you use these activities to make an eternal impact? Should you focus on fewer activities so that you can make them more meaningful?

HOLDING ON

TO UNANSWERED QUESTIONS

"He has made everything beautiful in its time. He has also set eternity in the hearts of men; yet they cannot fathom what God has done from beginning to end." **Ecclesiastes 3:11**

People are always asking questions. This curiosity and desire for knowledge begins when we are young. As soon as a toddler begins sounding out his or her first words, it is only a matter of time before the questions start flooding out. *Why? Where? What? When? How?* Anyone who has attempted to answer a toddler's question knows that oftentimes the child follows up with another question, and then another. Sometimes it can seem like children are only asking questions playfully to try and get attention. However, a study done by researchers at the University of Michigan found that when children ask questions, even if they are simply repeating the word *why*, most times they genuinely want an explanation.

Asking big questions has done us a great deal of good as a society. It has led to several medical breakthroughs and scientific discoveries. But in this age of information—when we can simply pull out our cell phones, do a quick search, and settle almost any argument—it seems as if it is becoming more and more difficult for us to accept the fact that there is great mystery in our theology. Open your Bible and read Ecclesiastes 3:11. Solomon wrote, "He has made everything beautiful in its time. He has also set eternity in the hearts of men; yet they cannot fathom what God has done from beginning to end." All people are born with eternity in their hearts. This is why so many people attest to thinking about God, wondering about heaven, and even praying before they ever put their faith in Jesus. It is because God has placed an awareness of eternity inside of all of us. He has made us mindful of something more than our eyes can see or our hands can touch, but we are prevented from wrapping our minds around it completely.

When we were children it was in our nature to look at our surroundings and ask questions. This was how we learned about the world around us. But just because we asked the questions does not mean that we were always ready for the answers. For example, a child will ask where babies come from before he or she can comprehend the answer. This is the situation many of us find ourselves in. We have a collection of unanswered questions about life and faith and infinite other things, and in this day and age it is hard to come to terms with the fact that every answer is not waiting to be found on Google. But we must take to heart the words of Solomon.

God has put an awareness of eternity inside of our hearts, but we have not fully understood it. This has left us with a lot of questions, and understandably so. But we must not hold these questions against God, as if He owed us an answer every time we ask "Why?" or "How?" As is the case with toddlers, we are often asking questions before we are ready or capable of processing the answers. As Charles Spurgeon once put it, "I bless God for a religion which I cannot understand. If I could perfectly understand it I would not believe it to be divine; for I should be sure it did not come from the infinite God if I could grasp it and comprehend it."

THINK ABOUT IT
What are some unanswered questions about life and faith that you find yourself holding on to?

PRAY ABOUT IT
Pray that God would guard your heart against any bitterness and resentment as you live with these unanswered questions.

DO SOMETHING ABOUT IT
Take a moment to jot down your unanswered questions onto a piece of paper and then take them to someone you trust, like a parent or pastor, and ask them for their thoughts.

DAY 15

LETTING GO

OF YOUR PAST

"Brothers, I do not consider myself yet to have taken hold of it. But one thing I do: Forgetting what is behind and straining toward what is ahead, I press on toward the goal to win the prize for which God has called me heavenward in Christ Jesus." **Philippians 3:13-14**

LETTING GO OF YOUR PAST

Have you ever seen the movie *Invictus*? It is based on a true story in which the president of South Africa, Nelson Mandela, unites the country through rugby. You see, South Africa had a long history of racism. Nelson Mandela, who had spent most of his life in prison because he protested against racism, was the first black president. He wanted to encourage South Africa to let go of its past of racism and embrace a future of unity. This was no easy task because even in rugby the black South Africans would cheer against the all white South African rugby team, the Springboks. So, Nelson Mandela thought that if the Springboks won the 1995 Rugby World Cup, then that would help unite the country. He shared his plan with the captain of the Springboks, Francois Pienaar. Together they worked to ensure the team was ready to win the World Cup. At one point the Springboks visited the prison where President Mandela has spent most of his life. Pienaar is amazed that Mandela, "could spend thirty years in a tiny cell, and come out ready to forgive the people who put him there."

Our past can either drive us to succeed or hold us back. The difference in how our past motivates us depends on what we do with our past. Do we hold on to it or do we let it go?

Read Philippians 3:13-14. Paul has had a shaky past. He called himself the sinner of sinners. He had spent a long time studying scripture and trying to follow the law. He had made it his job to judge others and make sure people were not disobeying God. He had even led a movement to kill Christians because he thought they were teaching a bad religion. All that changed when he encountered Christ. Now when Paul encountered the light of Jesus (Read Acts 9:1-19 to learn about Paul's conversion) he looked at his past and saw how dark it was. I am sure he felt ashamed. That is the natural, human reaction when we look at our past in light of the future with Christ. However, eventually Paul saw it for was it was, in the past. He let it go and began journeying with Christ toward his future.

LETTING GO OF YOUR PAST

The movie *Invictus* is named after a poem of the same name by William Ernest Henley. Invictus is a Latin word meaning "unconquered" or "undefeated." You are not defeated by your past.

How do you let go of your past? You give and accept forgiveness. Now, you may think, "I don't have the strength to do that." You are right! You don't, but God does. He can give you the strength to forgive. He can give you the ability to let go of the past, forgive, and move on.

The last two lines of the poem Invictus says this, "I am the master of my fate: I am the captain of my soul." Make Jesus Christ the master of your fate and the captain of your soul. He will help you let go of your past and move on to freedom.

THINK ABOUT IT

If Christ has the power to rise from the dead don't you think He can give you the power to let go of your past and forgive?

PRAY ABOUT IT

Spend some time asking God to show you things in your past you have not let go of. Ask God to give you his strength to let your past go so you can go with him into freedom.

DO SOMETHING ABOUT IT

Write or talk with someone whom you have hurt in your past. Ask that person for forgiveness.

LETTING GO

OF YOUR PAIN

"But he said to me, 'My grace is sufficient for you, for my power is made perfect in weakness.' Therefore I will boast all the more gladly about my weaknesses, so that Christ's power may rest on me." **2 Corinthians 12:9**

LETTING GO OF YOUR PAIN

Chances are you have seen a comedy in which the character gets electrocuted. Usually it happens when he or she grabs a frayed wire. The character goes all bug-eyed and his or her hair shoots straight up like porcupine quills. When people watch these sorts of scenes many of them are probably thinking to themselves, *why not just let go of the wire?* It seems to be a simple solution. Let go of the thing that is causing you pain. But in reality it is not so easy. When electricity passes through a person's body it interferes with the nervous system, causing the muscles to contract, and prevents the person from controlling his or her motor functions. Essentially, when it comes to electricity the greater the pain the harder it is to let go.

When characters get electrocuted they never seem as if they "delight in it." Even in comedies, where the scene is designed to make the audience laugh, the character never sits back after being electrocuted and "boasts" in the experience. That would seem a little crazy, right? And yet in 2 Corinthians 12:9-10 Paul said that he would "delight" in his pain and "boast" in his weaknesses. Paul wrote, "But he said to me, 'My grace is sufficient for you, for my power is made perfect in weakness.' Therefore I will boast all the more gladly about my weaknesses, so that Christ's power may rest on me. That is why, for Christ's sake, I delight in weaknesses, in insults, in hardships, in persecutions, in difficulties. For when I am weak, then I am strong."

Paul wrote the majority of the New Testament, and not once did he claim being a Christ-follower equated to living the easy life. Even heroes of the faith like Paul experience pain in their lives. But God gave Paul an insight which he then shared with all of us: God's grace and power is greater than any pain we hold on to, whether it is the emotional pain of insults or the physical pain of persecution or anything in between. Nothing is so great that God cannot lift it. That is one reason why Paul said that he would delight and boast in his pain and weakness, because he knew that moments of pain and weakness were moments when God showed up in a powerful way.

LETTING GO OF YOUR PAIN

When we let go of the pain in our lives, whether physical or relational or spiritual, we start to discover the sufficiency and power of Christ taking its place, filling the spaces and cracks left behind by the broken pieces that once filled us. The trouble is, just like with electricity, the greater the pain the harder it seems to let go. The good news is this: God's power is perfected in our weakness. When we are unable to release different kinds of pain from our grip, God promises his strength. We must remember that it is difficult to take hold of the rest and grace and power Jesus promised if our hands are busy holding on to pain. Letting go of the pain does not mean pretending that we never felt it. Rather, letting go of pain is a step toward healing. It is an act of faith, letting go and entrusting these personal moments and painful experiences to the care of God.

THINK ABOUT IT

What are some ways you can begin letting go of pain and relying on God's grace today?

PRAY ABOUT IT

Ask God to make His power perfect in the midst of your pain and weakness.

DO SOMETHING ABOUT IT

Follow Paul's example and find a friend or family member and boast in your weakness as you share with them Christ's power.

LETTING GO

OF YOUR UNFORGIVENESS

"Then Peter came to Jesus and asked, "Lord, how many times shall I forgive my brother when he sins against me? Up to seven times?" Jesus answered, "I tell you, not seven times, but seventy-seven times."
Matthew 18:21-22

LETTING GO OF YOUR UNFORGIVENESS

Control. No one wants to give it up. Why? It's because we usually associate control with power. One who has control over an object has power over it. A basketball player with good control of the ball has the power to play well. A driver with control over their car has the power to drive it wherever he or she wishes to go. Women and children who are trafficked in the sex trade have no power because all control has been taken from them.

Unforgiveness seems like power. As long as we maintain it, we have control. We want someone to pay for what's been done to us, and if we forgive that person, we might lose the power to make someone pay. Right? In reality, when we don't forgive, we are allowing sin to have control over us—not forgiving enslaves us to sins including unrighteous anger and bitterness; we give power to sin. But, forgiveness takes control away from our sin and the sin of our offender and places it back in the hands of Christ; our offender no longer has the power to control our emotions, reactions, or futures. Previously we discussed our need to forgive based on the forgiveness we received from Christ. Truly, Christ is our motivation to forgive others who have wronged us—to relinquish our right to "get back" at them.

Certainly forgiveness is not easy. But God does expect it of us. Read Matthew 18:21-22. The Jewish culture of Jesus' day claimed that forgiving someone three times was generous. When Peter asked Jesus if seven times was enough to forgive someone, he thought he was being more than generous to his offender. Jesus, however, quickly left Peter facing his inadequate reality. Jesus' response to Peter was not intended to give us an exact number of times that we are to forgive someone. Rather, Jesus pointed out that His disciples are to have a forgiving spirit that doesn't keep count of wrongs.

Eventually, we will all feel the sting of being sinned against and must deal with the effects for years to come, maybe even a lifetime. We may have to practically deal with the consequences, which may require difficult decisions on our part. But Jesus requires that we make those decisions based not on feelings of anger or bitterness but out of an attitude that releases control of vengeance to Him. If we are to follow Christ, we imitate His forgiveness and let go of that which prevents us from following Him with our whole heart, our whole mind, and our whole soul. If we are to follow Christ, we must let go of the sin of unforgiveness.

Fortunately Christ has not called us to do this out of our own power, for we cannot do something so righteous in human terms. He has sent the Holy Spirit to help us act in forgiveness and love our offenders when we don't feel forgiving.

THINK ABOUT IT

How can we act in a forgiving manner even when we aren't feeling compassion or forgiveness towards another?

PRAY ABOUT IT

Ask God to empower you to forgive those who have hurt you.

DO SOMETHING ABOUT IT

Look for one way that you can act in a forgiving manner towards someone who has hurt you this week, even if it's as simple as sending a text to say "Hello."

LETTING GO

OF YOUR PARENTS' DREAMS

"If anyone comes to me and does not hate father and mother, wife and children, brothers and sisters—yes, even their own life—such a person cannot be my disciple." **Luke 14:26**

LETTING GO OF YOUR PARENTS' DREAMS

Donna's dad is a doctor. Not a small town family doctor, rather he's a big time surgeon at the best hospital in the state. Her mom is a Registered Nurse and her sister is currently in medical school. Donna is in 11th grade and can already feel the pressure of joining the medical field with the rest of her family. She has no idea how to tell them she's feeling like God wants her to take a year off after High School to do mission work.

Craig did just what his parents wanted. He didn't even think about it really. He just did what was expected. Good grades, good college, good job… It wasn't until he was married and working as a Mechanical Engineer that he began to listen to God's voice telling him He has a bigger plan for his life. After months of prayer he felt certain that God wanted him to quit his job and go into ministry full time. When he told his parents, his dad got up and left the table without a word. When his dad finally returned his biggest argument was "You won't make any money!" Today Craig is in full time ministry and while he's not rich, he's full.

In Luke 14, Jesus was eating dinner at the home of a prominent Pharisee. While there, Jesus talked about the real sacrifice involved with following Him and said one of the most troubling quotes in all of the New Testament: "If anyone comes to me and does not hate father and mother, wife and children, brothers and sisters – yes, even their own life –such a person cannot be my disciple." Luke 14:26

It's not that you should be disobedient or disrespectful to your parents and Jesus certainly isn't giving you the right to hate your parents because they're cramping your style. But when you really choose the way of Jesus, "hate" might best describe what it looks like to the rest of the world.

In Jesus' time it was expected that young men would follow in their father's career path and learn the family trade. Young women would follow in their mother's footsteps becoming a wife and mother themselves. This was honoring to your father and mother. Doing something different was dishonoring and disrespectful. It might even be seen as hateful.

LETTING GO OF YOUR PARENTS' DREAMS

Today, things are a little different… but not much.

Taking up your cross and radically following Jesus is the kind of thing that doesn't make sense to the world. It goes right in the face of the American Dream: good grades, good college, good job, pretty wife, successful husband, big house, 3.2 children, a 401k and exotic vacations every year… all the things your parents worked hard for you to have.

The question is: What is God's plan for your life?

If you haven't already, begin praying that God would show you His plans for your life and try to begin having open conversations with your parents about your future. Some parents will be very open and receptive. Others will be more difficult. For that matter some of you will be open and receptive and some of you will be more difficult. Whatever the nature of your relationship with your parents and whatever the difference between God's plans and your parents' dreams for your life, here are some things you can do today:

- Submit to God. Whatever He requires, be prepared to give. The call to follow Jesus is a call to take up your own cross and follow Him.
- Let go of your parents' dreams for your life. You don't have to be a doctor because your parents want you to be.
- Also let go of your parents' curses on your life. If you happen to have a parent that puts you down, even unintentionally, know this: God made you in His image and loves you as His very own child.
- Forgive your parents. They're people too. Forgive them for their mistakes and for the dreams they may have pushed on you.
- Fear not. Where God calls, He provides. God knows what's best for you and wants what's best for you. Don't fear the consequences of following God.
- Check yourself. God's not calling you to shack up with your girlfriend or anything else against what the Bible says.
- Be honest with your parents and with yourself.

THINK ABOUT IT

Think about who your parents are. What was their home like growing up? What struggles did they have? What might be some of the underlying causes for why they act the way they act? How are you like them?

PRAY ABOUT IT

Give thanks for the parents God gave you. If your parents are no longer with you for whatever reason, thank God for the adult mentors in your life like your pastor or teacher who believes in you and loves you enough to have dreams for your life.

DO SOMETHING ABOUT IT

Decide today that you will not be defined by what others say you are but by what God says you are: His beloved.

LETTING GO
OF YOUR DREAMS

"'Truly I tell you,' Jesus replied, 'no one who has left home or brothers or sisters or mother or father or children or fields for me and the gospel will fail to receive a hundred times as much in this present age; homes, brothers, sisters, mothers, children and fields – along with persecutions – and in the age to come eternal life.'" **Mark 10:29-30**

LETTING GO OF YOUR DREAMS

Emma decided to give up her dream. She had wanted to be a college cheerleader since she started cheerleading in 6th grade. Then, as a sophomore she wanted something different. She wanted to feel closer to Jesus. She couldn't quite explain it to her friends, who were all cheerleaders, but she was not satisfied. After she quit cheerleading she thought it wouldn't be a big deal. She would have more time to go to church, hang out with her youth group friends whom she hadn't seen in 6 months because of cheerleading practices and games. But it was a big deal. Her closest friends, who were all cheerleaders, stopped being her friends. For the first time she found herself not popular, but instead hanging out at home on Friday nights.

Read Mark 10:28-31. Remember several days ago you read about the rich young ruler who was invited to follow Jesus, but didn't because he couldn't give up his riches. After the rich young ruler decided not to give up his dream to follow Christ the disciples were perplexed. Unlike that rich guy, they had given up everything to follow Christ. They had left their family, their jobs, and their friends. It wasn't an easy thing to do but they did. What would their future hold?

Notice that Jesus doesn't promise everything will be easy when you give up your dreams and follow him. The fact is: Following Jesus will not always make your life easy. You might lose friends, lose family members, and lose some comforts that you are used to. But even with all that you may lose, Jesus promises so much more.

Jesus said you would receive a hundred times what you gave up. Did you give up your dreams? The dream that God has for you will be 100 times better! How can that be? When we allow God to lead us in the direction that He wants us to go our old dreams seem to be nothing compared to what God has in store.

Remember Millard Fuller? His dream was to become rich and he quickly reached his dream, but when he gave up his dream (and his money) God led him to a whole lot more. Not only did he start Habitat for Humanity and build over 500,000 homes for 2.5 million people around the world. He also received 50 honorary degrees. He received two awards from the President of the United States. A totally different life than he could have ever dreamed.

Even Emma gained more following Christ. She found a whole lot of new friends. People she used to think weren't good enough for her. These new friends were more loyal and fun than her old friends. Her reputation changed too. She went from being seen as a popular cheerleader to a person who showed compassion to others. She was even asked to preach on youth Sunday at her church.

Following Christ is not easy. It may cost you your friends, your job, or your dreams, but it is so much better. When you follow Christ you start acting like Christ. Showing compassion to people in need of compassion, not worrying about things you don't need to worry about, and showing love to the unlovable. Have you had a hard time since you gave up everything and followed Christ? Hang in there! Christ is transforming you into something beyond your dreams.

THINK ABOUT IT

How is God changing your life now that you have started following him? Are you having a hard time now that you let go of your old dreams?

PRAY ABOUT IT

Ask God for comfort if you are having a hard time with your new life in Christ. Ask God to transform you and give you a new dream.

DO SOMETHING ABOUT IT

While you are waiting for a new dream go and act like Christ. Sit with the kid who eats lunch alone. Get to know that person.

LETTING GO

OF YOUR REPUTATION

"The Spirit himself testifies with our spirit that we are God's children. Now if we are children, then we are heirs—heirs of God and co-heirs with Christ, if indeed we share in his sufferings in order that we may also share in his glory."

Romans 8:16-17

LETTING GO OF YOUR REPUTATION

Back in 2008, an Australian man named Ian Usher made international news after putting his life up for sale on eBay. He was 44 at the time and had just been divorced from his wife. He left a note on his webpage that read, "I have had enough of my life! I don't want it anymore!" The eBay sale included his car, his motorcycle, his jet ski, his house, and his job, among other things. He even threw in his friends. You are probably wondering how someone could put his friendships up for sale. Well, it turns out whoever won the bid for Mr. Usher's life would also receive an introduction to his friends. He received many fake bids before finally selling his life to someone for around 339,000 Australian dollars, or approximately 307,400 US dollars. Mr. Usher spent the next two years travelling, then he wrote a book about selling his life on eBay, and he just recently sold Disney the rights to make his story into a movie.

Ian Usher's marriage came to a tragic end, at which point he decided that he wanted a fresh start. This might seem like an exciting idea to a lot of people, selling everything and starting over, but Scripture shares with us a much more exciting notion. Open your Bible and read Romans 8:16-17. Paul wrote, "The Spirit himself testifies with our spirit that we are God's children. Now if we are children, then we are heirs—heirs of God and co-heirs with Christ, if indeed we share in his sufferings in order that we may also share in his glory."

Paul was talking about one of the most profound joys of the true Gospel, which is that we have been given a new beginning, a fresh identity, and a sterling reputation before God in Christ. And this new reputation, as children of God and co-heirs with Christ, outshines any former reputation that we might have had. You might have been known as the guy who partied hard or the girl who made poor choices in relationships, but in this passage Paul reminds all of us that the Spirit of God testifies on our behalf that we are now children of God. Who better to make that declaration than God Himself?

Ian Usher sold his life, which included his job and most of his belongings, to the highest bidder. From the outside looking in it appears as if he may have been attempting to sell away his former reputation and identity in order to start again. Scripture tells us that God is the highest bidder for our lives and that He has tied our identity to Christ. Paul said that if we are children of God then we are "heirs." That is our new identity, children and heirs. That is an identity Christ bought for us at the price of his very life. If you have placed your faith in Christ then you have a new identity before God and it is time to let go of your old reputation.

You do not have to resort to selling your life on eBay. Enjoy the freedom of letting go of your former reputation and finding your new identity in Christ. You are no longer the guy or girl who gets drunk every weekend. You are no longer the guy or girl who does not know how to say no. We are no longer the people who feel that we have to bend to every wish or demand of our peers.

THINK ABOUT IT

What are some ways you can let go of your former reputation so that you can continue growing in your identity as a co-heir with Christ and child of God?

PRAY ABOUT IT

Take a moment and thank God for the reputation He offers us in Christ, and then ask him to help you live according to that reputation.

DO SOMETHING ABOUT IT

As you take steps to let go of your former reputation, make a deliberate effort to share the good news of your new identity with the people in your life.

LETTING GO

OF YOUR FAME

"Do nothing out of selfish ambition or vain conceit. Rather, in humility value others above yourselves." **Philippians 2:3**

LETTING GO OF YOUR FAME

There's a phenomenon going on within most youth groups today, an unwritten statute so widely accepted that few would even argue against it. It's a means of choosing the best, the fastest, the most important, the most popular and the coolest students in the group and placing them in the forefront. It gives those chosen the seat of honor, figuratively and sometimes literally. The rest are relegated to what's left. Of course, we want the prominent place for ourselves.

We see this play out in a competition that has long been a mainstay of teenage culture. Whether in a youth group or just hanging out with a bunch of friends, I bet you can tell me what happens before piling into a vehicle… someone calls *Shotgun!* Different youth groups have different rules for *Shotgun*. They usually include things like: the vehicle must be in sight, the group must be moving to the vehicle with intentions to get in, and the first to call "Shotgun!" gets to ride in the front seat.

Of course right now you're probably thinking, "It's not like that. I don't think I'm better than anyone. It's just about riding up front." Fair enough, let's not be overly dramatic. But with that simple scene in mind, let's check God's word.

In Philippians 2, Paul presents a wonderful case for imitating Christ in his humility. If he were writing for a newspaper, verse 3 would be the headline: "Do nothing out of selfish ambition or vain conceit. Rather, in humility value others above yourselves." There are a lot of big words in that little verse, so let's take a look at them one-by-one:

Selfish: interested in yourself.

Ambition: goals and desires.

Selfish Ambition: interested in your own goals and desires.

Vain: hopeless, proud.

Conceit: arrogance.

LETTING GO OF YOUR FAME

Vain Conceit: hopeless, proud arrogance

So Paul says not to do anything out of an interest in your own goals and desires or out of hopeless pride or arrogance. In other words, stop looking out for just yourself. Paul goes on to say "In humility value others above yourselves." Humility is a tough word to define, but it basically means considering others better than you.

Look out for the interest of others and consider others better than yourself.

Who sits where in a car is really not a big issue. The thing with always calling *Shotgun!* is that it reveals a bigger problem: we almost always look out for ourselves first. Think about the time you went white water rafting with the youth group, when you went into the room to get paddles, helmets and vests, you went for the best looking gear didn't you? Think about the lunchroom yesterday. Did you look to find a seat with your friends or did you try to find someone who didn't have a friend to sit with?

As it turns out, when we begin thinking about our daily routine, a lot of what we do is focused on ourselves, our own wants, our own desires, our own popularity, our own fame. That's not how Jesus was. And it's not how we're supposed to be. The first step in letting go of your own fame is realizing your own selfishness. Be intentional, in everything you do, to think of others as better than yourself.

THINK ABOUT IT

Think about your daily routine: where you sit, the people you hang with, what you say and what you do. Think of the times you put yourself first and think of the opportunities you have to put others first.

PRAY ABOUT IT

Pray that God would open your eyes to your own selfishness and that God would open your eyes to the interests of others.

DO SOMETHING ABOUT IT

Consider others better than yourself and treat them as though they really are.

LETTING GO

OF THE NOISE

"Remember the Sabbath day by keeping it holy... For in six days the Lord made the heavens and the earth, the sea, and all that is in them, but he rested on the seventh day. Therefore the Lord blessed the Sabbath day and made it holy." **Exodus 20:8,11**

LETTING GO OF THE NOISE

Bernie Krause has spent 25+ years traveling around the world and recording sounds of nature's creatures and environments. He and his company Wild Sanctuary have produced at least 50 albums and sound backgrounds for museums, zoos and the like. In his book *Into a Wild Sanctuary* Krause writes: "In 1968, when I first began my odyssey, I could record for about 15 hours and capture about one hour of usable sound – a ratio of about 15 to 1. Now it takes nearly 2,000 hours to obtain one hour of untainted natural sound."

That was written in 1998. Today it's worse.

Humanity has filled every available space with visible or audible noise: iPods in every pocket, televisions in every room, paved roads on every piece of land, dams on every stream, billboards on every highway, magazines at every checkout counter and advertisements on every Facebook page. Bigger, faster, louder and more is the cost of progress. Immediately after God rescued Israel from slavery in Egypt and made them a free nation (not just a small family) God gave them the first thing every free nation needs: the Law. And one of the principles explicit in the Law is to rest, or take a Sabbath.

Exodus 20: 8-11 says, "Remember the Sabbath day by keeping it holy. Six days you shall labor and do all your work, but the seventh day is a Sabbath to the Lord your God. On it you shall not do any work, neither you, nor your son or daughter, nor your male or female servant, nor your animals, nor any foreigner residing in your towns. For in six days the Lord made the heavens and the earth, the sea, an all that is in them, but he rested on the seventh day. Therefore the Lord blessed the Sabbath day and made it holy."

God knew the temptation Israel would face when they moved into the land of milk and honey, the deception of wealth and the temptation to accumulate more. Practicing a weekly Sabbath helped ensure God's people did not become slaves to economic growth as they were in Egypt. And it wasn't just a weekly Sabbath that the Law required. In Leviticus 25, God commanded Israel to give the land a rest every seventh year. Furthermore, God set in place a year of Jubilee to occur every seventh yearly Sabbath (every 49 years) in which all debts were forgiven, prisoners released and slates were cleaned.

Practicing Sabbath ensures that we…

Stop.

Breathe.

Don't become a slave to the noise.

Letting go of the noise means intentionally setting aside the things that constantly lobby for your attention at the expense of time with God. This is a simple concept to understand but an inevitably difficult one to live. It requires taking an honest inventory of your life and the things that fill it, then intentionally making changes to your lifestyle to make time and space for God to speak to you and through you.

THINK ABOUT IT

Think about the things in your life screaming for your attention. Make a list. It might be electronics or peers, maybe the things you look at or take part in. Name the noise in your life that is making it difficult for you to hear God.

PRAY ABOUT IT

Pray that God would help you remove that noise from your life.

DO SOMETHING ABOUT IT

Remove the noise that you can remove. Change your habits. Unplug your TV. You can't remove the billboards on the highway but you can throw your phone in a lake. Yeah people might think you're weird. So what? There's never been a person in history to hear clearly from God whose peers didn't think they were weird.

LETTING GO

OF THE CRITICS

"Blessed are the meek, for they will inherit the earth." **Matthew 5:5**

LETTING GO OF THE CRITICS

Has your mom ever said to you, "When you are pointing your finger, you have three pointing straight back at you!" Moms usually say that when you are being too critical of someone. You know, sometimes we can point at someone and complain about how critical he or she is of us when in reality we are just as critical of others. Often, as the critic, what we have to let go of is ourselves so that we can clearly listen to God and others.

Did you watch *Mr. Rogers' Neighborhood* when you were little? Did you know that Mr. Rogers was a Presbyterian minister? He told a story one time about hearing a sermon while he was in seminary. He said it was the worst sermon he had ever heard. The preacher broke every rule of delivering a sermon. He felt it was just a big waste of time. After the sermon he overheard the woman next to him crying saying, "That is exactly what I needed to hear." How could Mr. Rogers feel like it was a waste of time and the woman next to him get so much out of it? He concluded that it was all about the attitude they brought with them to church that morning. He came with a critical spirit and she came with a spirit of need.

Read Matthew 5:5. This is just one verse in seven verses that make up what is called the Beatitudes. This was the first thing Jesus taught His disciples in the Sermon on the Mount. They are steps we have to take in order to grow closer to Christ. Sometimes in order to get close to an important person we have to show how awesome we are, but the Beatitudes teach us that we have to humble ourselves and recognize our need for God in order to grow closer to God. This one beatitude reminds us to be meek. Now, we often equate meekness with weakness, but that is not what Jesus is saying here. Jesus is telling us (His disciples) that there is no reason we should think of ourselves as better than someone else. Paul reminds us in Romans 3:23 that, "all have sinned and fall short of the glory of God." We are all on level playing field.

So if we are meek and don't show our awesomeness how can we inherit the earth? You don't inherit something by working for it. Your inheritance is based on your relationship. When you have a relationship with Christ you are God's child and therefore receive an inheritance from God. You don't need to be critical because that doesn't get you anything. Be satisfied that God loves you. As a child of God, love the people your Heavenly Father loves! When you do, you have no need to be critical.

Are you becoming meek? Have you let go of your critical attitude? It is time for you to do that. It is the way to freedom, to an abundant life. When you allow God to change you from critical to meek you are able to be a good neighbor and inherit the earth.

THINK ABOUT IT
How many times do you have a critical thought or say a critical word about someone?

PRAY ABOUT IT
It is hard to let go of a critical attitude. God has the power to take that attitude away. Spend some time today confessing this attitude to God and ask God to change you.

DO SOMETHING ABOUT IT
If you have been critical of someone recently and they know about it, you need to go and ask for forgiveness.

DAY 6

LETTING GO

OF CONVENIENCE

"Then Jesus said to his disciples, 'If anyone would come after me, he must deny himself and take up his cross and follow me... What good will it be for a man if he gains the whole world, yet he forfeits his soul? Or what can a man give in exchange for his soul?'" **Matthew 16:24, 26**

LETTING GO OF CONVENIENCE

Daniel was doing really well for a person in his twenties. He was living in a big apartment, driving around in an expensive Mercedes SUV, and making good money as a lawyer for the United Nations Office on Drugs and Crime. One day he met a lady who had been kidnapped and taken to Japan as a slave prostitute. As he talked with her he noticed a tattoo on her neck and asked her where she got it. She told Daniel that it was put on her as a sign that she was someone's property. Following that conversation Daniel spent several days praying, wondering how he could help people in a way that would last, in a way that could not be taken away or undone. As he was praying he received an email from a friend about an organization that plants churches all over Peru. Daniel took his time thinking it over, and after several months of prayer he made his decision. He quit his job at the UN, took a major pay decrease, sold his Mercedes, and started working with mission groups in Peru.

Open your Bible and read Matthew 16:24 and 26. In this passage Matthew, a disciple of Jesus, recorded the words of our Savior. "If anyone would come after me, he must deny himself and take up his cross and follow me. What good will it be for a man if he gains the whole world, yet he forfeits his soul? Or what can a man give in exchange for his soul?" This is a truth that Daniel knows well. He was living a life of luxury and financial security. He had all the conveniences that a young person in his twenties could ask for, but over time he realized that being a Christ-follower is not summed up in a life of convenience. On the contrary, being a Christian, at least according to the founder of Christianity, means taking up a cross. After a lot of prayer Daniel realized that in order for him to live the life he was created to live he would need to let go of his expensive belongings, his fancy job, and the conveniences of wealth and start a new life as a missionary and church planter. And Daniel was happy to do that because, after all, what conveniences could this world possibly offer to us that would be worth our souls?

You may have heard the old saying, "If something is worth having, it is worth fighting for." It appears that many people today have decided that something is only worth having if you do not have to fight for it. It is only worth our time and effort if it saves us time and effort. But we have things backwards and upside down. Jesus did not preach a gospel of convenience. As we see in Matthew 16:24 and 26, Jesus preached a gospel of sacrifice. Jesus' sacrifice is what saves us, and a life of sacrifice, not convenience, is what we are called to live. God is not going to call everyone to make the same decision Daniel made, but if you read Daniel's story and think to yourself that you could never leave a high paying job and luxurious lifestyle, then you are holding too tightly on to convenience and it is time to let go. Listen to Jesus' words about carrying a cross and remember that he was talking to you. A life that is convenience-focused does not mesh with a life that is Kingdom-focused, so be willing to let go of convenience for the sake of the Gospel.

THINK ABOUT IT

What are some ways you can begin letting go of a convenience-focused mindset and grabbing hold of the Kingdom-focused attitude of which Jesus spoke?

PRAY ABOUT IT

Pray and ask God to help you free your hands of conveniences so that you can pick up your cross and follow Christ.

DO SOMETHING ABOUT IT

As a way of taking a step forward, choose at least one convenience in your life and spend at least one week without it.

LETTING GO

OF SELFISHNESS

"You, my brothers, were called to be free. But do not use your freedom to indulge the sinful nature; rather, serve one another in love. The entire law is summed up in a single command: "Love your neighbor as yourself." If you keep on biting and devouring each other, watch out or you will be destroyed by each other." **Galatians 5:13-15**

LETTING GO OF SELFISHNESS

When we live at home with our parents, they can infuriate us to such great lengths that we often say something like, "I can't wait until I'm on my own and can do whatever I want!" And it's true that when we become financially stable enough to live in our own place and pay our own bills that we can usually make our own house rules. The problem is that when we have the responsibilities of an adult—paying bills, going to work, making your own health decisions, buying your own toilet paper—we have to begin to act like an adult. We can't call in sick whenever we don't feel like going to work. We have to do our work assignments or we will get fired. With freedom comes the responsibility to know how to use it wisely. Or, as Spiderman's uncle said, "With great power comes great responsibility."

The same idea is true for Christians. We are no longer required to follow the Law in order to obtain salvation. Jesus did that for us. We live in the freedom of His sacrifice. BUT, we are still expected to obey the commands of God because they tell us how to please Him, how to worship Him, and how to walk in the righteousness of Christ. Obedience does not save us, but it is the fruit of true salvation. Therefore, Jesus stated in Matthew 22:37-40 that all of the laws can be summed up by loving God with all of your heart, soul, and mind and loving your neighbor as yourself.

Read Galatians 5:13-15. Paul restated Jesus' teaching in this passage by emphasizing the importance of loving and serving one another. Paul emphasized that our freedom as Christians does not give us the right to do whatever we want. Rather, our freedom brings responsibility to walk according to the righteous calling of the Lord; and that calling is to love God and love our neighbors.

What is the opposite of love? Is it hate? Or is it selfishness? Godly love can most simply be defined by an unselfish concern for the best interest of another. So, if we are concerned for our own best interest at the expense of another, we are doing the opposite of love; we are being selfish, or hateful. We discussed having an attitude of selflessness a couple of weeks ago and how it demonstrates the sacrificial nature of the gospel lived out in our lives. Developing an attitude of selflessness and acting on that attitude requires us to love others as we do ourselves. Of course, this love isn't something that we can do on our own, especially for those hard-to-love people.

The beauty of loving others is the same as salvation: it has to come from Christ because we cannot do it on our own. But we can take steps to allow Christ to open our hearts and minds. It begins with honest confession and prayer about our selfish tendencies. Then, we can ask God to love others through us because we are inadequate to do it on our own.

THINK ABOUT IT

Who have you intentionally or unintentionally hurt because you weren't acting in a loving manner towards him or her?

PRAY ABOUT IT

Confess the ways you have acted in selfish hatred toward others. Ask God to love through you and to develop a love for others in your heart.

DO SOMETHING ABOUT IT

Ask yourself in every decision, "How am I demonstrating the selfless love of Christ to others?" Intentionally seek ways to practically demonstrate love to other people, including praying for those toward whom you don't "feel" loving.

LETTING GO
OF WHAT IF

"Do not be anxious about anything, but in everything, by prayer and petition, with thanksgiving, present your requests to God. And the peace of God, which transcends all understanding, will guard your hearts and your minds in Christ Jesus. Finally, brothers, whatever is true, whatever is noble, whatever is right, whatever is pure, whatever is lovely, whatever is admirable—if anything is excellent or praiseworthy—think about such things."

Philippians 4:6-8

LETTING GO OF WHAT IF

If humans had no emotions and could solely think in terms of logic, then worry would never be an issue. Like the Vulcans in *Star Trek*, we could go about our daily tasks without the problems of anxiety or worry butting in on our thoughts. We could face any daunting task with a steady mind and endure suffering with all the logic of an encyclopedia because we could suppress our worry with the mental strength of the Vulcans. We do not have the luxury of being taught how to suppress our emotions like a Vulcan, though, and even the most logical of thoughts can bring little comfort in the face of uncertainty and worry. But we know what they know: the mind is powerful.

In fact, the mind is the main battleground for warring against the uncertainties of life that can cause us great anxiety. The mind is the place where thoughts and ideas become beliefs and actions. If Satan can get us to lose our focus on the truth about God and His purpose in our lives, then we can lose our effectiveness as a witness for Christ. Read Philippians 4:6-9. Paul told the Philippian church to not be anxious about anything. Rather, they were to pray to God about everything and trust Him to work on their behalf. Paul then said in verse 7 that the peace of God would guard their hearts and minds. Notice that Paul didn't say that external circumstances would change or even that we could control worry ourselves. God is the one who can guard our minds. It is no mistake, then, that the next two verses spell out what the Philippians should be thinking about—the things of God.

We can simply tell ourselves, or each other, not to worry, but the battle to take charge of our minds is one that we must perpetually fight with God's help. Paul could have said, "Be anxious about nothing" and ended his discourse about worry right then and there. But he didn't because he knew that the battle is bigger than our ability. The peace of God will guard our minds when we ask Him to do so. We must confess our anxiety to God and then meditate on Him and His word.

God created our minds, and when we meditate on Him and His word, we can use His truths to logically and biblically give our minds, full of worry and anxiety, over to the capable arms of God. Our minds are an intense battleground, but when we fill them up with God, there is no room for anxiety. By meditating on Him we are reminding ourselves of His trustworthy character and His sovereign care over us. Then, we can live with the peace of God guarding our minds against the paralyzing fear that creeps into our lives.

THINK ABOUT IT
What things have you been focusing on instead of God and His Word?

PRAY ABOUT IT
Confess your fears and ask God to guard your mind concerning them.

DO SOMETHING ABOUT IT
Memorize and meditate on Isaiah 26:3. Recite it when anxiety creeps into your thoughts. Begin memorizing Scripture to help combat particular fears in your life.

LETTING GO

OF WHAT'S FAIR

"Then the master called the servant in, 'You wicked servant,' he said, 'I canceled all that debt of yours because you begged me to.'"
Matthew 18:32

LETTING GO OF WHAT'S FAIR

Have you ever seen the President in person? Regardless of your political leanings, seeing the President of the United States would be really cool. Now imagine if you were one of the President's trusted advisors. How cool would that be? You would get to go in and out of the White House anytime you wanted. You may even get to fly on Air Force One!

Well, a guy named Chuck Colson got to do all that. He was a good friend and advisor to Richard Nixon during his presidency. Unfortunately, Chuck Colson would do anything for Richard Nixon, which got him mixed up in a BIG scandal called Watergate. He did things for Nixon that put him in jail. At some point while he was hanging out with the President, Colson felt he was missing something. A friend introduced him to Jesus. Now, Colson knew all the bad things that he had done. He did not try to hide them, but he knew that Jesus' sacrifice had taken his sins away. Colson was a free man in Christ even when sitting in prison. His life would never be the same after prison.

Read Matthew 18:23-35. This story could be called the story of the hypocrite. Here is this guy who has just been given a break, but wouldn't give the same break to someone else. What? Don't you hate hypocrites? You could probably point to several people in your life right now who have been hypocritical. But not you, right? Read this story again. This is a pretty harsh story from Jesus, but it is important to know that God really expects you to treat others the way He has treated you.

Several days ago you read about the gospel of Christ treating you unfairly in a good way. You were not punished for the sin you committed. Christ took that punishment so that you can have a deep, loving relationship with your Heavenly Father. God's mercy is a wonderful gift. Have you given others that same mercy? Letting go of what's fair means you treat people the way you have been treated by God. You show abundant mercy to others.

Chuck Colson went from hanging out with the President to hanging out with prisoners. Chuck could have thought, "I'm better than these prisoners! They deserve to be in here more than I do!" But he didn't. He knew that God had forgiven him of his sins and these prisoners were sinners just like he was. So what did he do when he got out of prison? Did he go back into politics? Did he try to gain back the power he once had? No! He started a prison ministry called Prison Fellowship.

Prison Fellowship reaches out to prisoners, ex-prisoners, and their families by sharing the gospel and helping them get back on their feet in 112 countries. You may have even given toys or money for their program, Angel Tree, which helps provide Christmas presents for children who have a parent in jail.

Chuck Colson did the opposite of the hypocrite in Jesus' story. He let go of what was fair and showed mercy. Have you let go of what's fair? Are you showing mercy and kindness to others even if they don't deserve it? You need to! Jesus' story reminds us how important it is to show mercy to others because so much mercy has been shown to us.

THINK ABOUT IT
Spend some time thinking about who in your life needs to be shown mercy even though they don't deserve it.

PRAY ABOUT IT
Ask God to give you strength to show mercy to that person or persons. Ask God to show ways you can show mercy to them.

DO SOMETHING ABOUT IT
Go show mercy to that person. Find some way you can be kind to him or her.

DAY 2

LETTING GO

OF WORLDLY CONFIDENCE

"Not that we are competent in ourselves to claim anything for ourselves, but our competence comes from God. He has made us competent as ministers of a new covenant—not of the letter but of the Spirit; for the letter kills, but the Spirit gives life." **2 Corinthians 3:5-6**

LETTING GO OF WORLDLY CONFIDENCE

Failing at something can be one of the most helpful learning experiences of our lives. But it can also be one of the most heartbreaking. When the entire world around you seems to be succeeding with barely any effort but you are stuck behind in your mundane world, you can feel like a failure. When it seems that God has shone down favor on everyone but you, you can feel forgotten. And when your friends have spiritual gifts that garner lots of attention on stage and you are sitting in the church basement praying that the copy machine would just work this one time, you feel inadequate for God's service—that maybe He doesn't need you after all.

Well, that's actually true for everyone. God doesn't need any of us—neither the people on stage nor the ones in the basement. There's nothing good about us that He didn't give us—skills, spiritual gifts, appearances, talents, resources. It's all His. We are just His stewards. Be honest: Thinking about that truth stings a little bit, doesn't it? We want to think that we have a lot to offer, but the reality is that there is nothing in and of ourselves in which we can boast except that of the cross of Christ. When we can come to this realization, we can state with Paul in Galatians 6:14 that the world and all of its seeming riches and glory appeal to us no longer because we follow Christ and boast in His work in our lives.

Read 2 Corinthians 3:5-6. Are we inadequate? Yes. Are we sufficient? No. Is Christ inadequate? No. Is Christ sufficient? Yes. Dealing with the truth of our true identity as persons completely dependent on God for every good thing can be crippling. Our culture is so focused on achievement and personal goals that it is difficult for us to come to terms with the truth that we can place no confidence in those worldly idols. There is an appropriate place for high self-esteem, but that self-esteem is only in the right place when we view ourselves through Christ. And He is who determines our self-worth. It is not our abilities that give us confidence. It is not what we can attain in this world that gives us confidence. The truth is that the saving power of Christ has set us free and claimed us as His children—children of the Creator of the universe! And that truth is accompanied by the realization that His power is at work in our lives through His abundant grace, and those truths are what form a healthy self-esteem for believers.

Yes, we are inadequate, but that is how God designed us. We are competent in Him alone. When we view ourselves in terms of worldly success we can feel like failures. But when we know that we are utterly dependent upon God and are sufficient in His power, we can have confidence in the One who is all-sufficient and we can trust in His work in our lives. Therefore, we don't have to feel like failures or walk around in a cloud of inadequacy. God has given us everything we need to succeed in obeying Him and walking according to His Word.

THINK ABOUT IT

Why is it such a shock to our system to consider that God doesn't need us?

PRAY ABOUT IT

Ask God to reveal His plan for you and to equip you to fulfill His calling on your life.

DO SOMETHING ABOUT IT

Take an honest look at what you are trying to accomplish with your life. Write down the ways in which you are relying on God every day compared to they ways in which you are relying on yourself.

LETTING GO

OF UNANSWERED QUESTIONS

"Oh, the depth of the riches of the wisdom and knowledge of God! How unsearchable his judgments, and his paths beyond tracing out! Who has known the mind of the Lord? Or who has been his counselor? For from him and through him and for him are all things. To him be the glory forever! Amen." **Romans 11:33-34,36**

LETTING GO OF UNANSWERED QUESTIONS

The movie *Cast Away* was released in 2000. It starred Tom Hanks as a FedEx employee whose plane crashes over the ocean and leaves him stranded on an uninhabited island. Many of us would probably imagine this as a vacation scenario, laying out on the beach all day and letting the cool water lap over our feet, but this is no holiday. He struggles for food, endures bad weather, and at one point he has to use an ice skate to remove one of his teeth. On top of all that, he is trying to get home to his longtime girlfriend. Three things keep him going during his stay on the island: a volleyball he talks to named "Wilson", a photo of his girlfriend, and an unopened FedEx package.

After four years on the island, he is finally able to construct a raft and set out to sea. He takes with him the photo of his girlfriend, Wilson, and the unopened package. While at sea Wilson falls into the ocean and is lost, after which Tom Hanks's character is found by a cargo ship and rescued. When he returns home he discovers that everyone thought he was dead, including his girlfriend who has married another man. With Wilson gone and his girlfriend married, he takes the unopened package he kept while he was stranded on the island and he delivers it. After letting go of the final thing that kept him going while on the island, Tom Hanks' character parks his car at a crossroads in the middle of nowhere. He opens up a map and places it on the hood of his car, and then walks into the middle of the intersection as if deciding what to do next. And then the credits roll.

In the case of the movie *Cast Away* the viewer feels as if he or she is left with more questions than answers, and some people left the theater displeased. But unanswered questions are a fact of life, even the Christian life. Read Romans 11:33-34 and 36. Paul wrote, "Oh, the depth of the riches of the wisdom and knowledge of God! How unsearchable his judgments, and his paths beyond tracing out! Who has known the mind of the Lord? Or who has been his counselor? For from him and through him and for him are all things. To him be the glory forever! Amen." Paul just gave us a wonderful attitude to imitate. Did you catch it? Paul seems overwhelmed by the deep and unsearchable mystery of God. And what does he do? He turns the mystery into a doxology, into worship!

Many people watch movies because they want something that is going to resolve. We want the story wrapped up with a happy conclusion that answers our questions, but the ending of *Cast Away* did not offer that. Likewise, God is not always going to answer our questions. And He likes it that way. Mystery is a part of His plan. As we see from Paul's words in Romans 11:33-34 and 36, the mystery and unanswered questions are meant, at least in part, to lead us to praise the Creator. There is nothing wrong with having questions. That is a part of being human. However, there is something wrong with holding on to these questions in such a way that they create bitterness or resentment. When holding on to questions builds walls between us and God, then it is time to let go.

THINK ABOUT IT

What are some unanswered questions that threaten to build walls between you and God?

PRAY ABOUT IT

After putting your finger on a few of these unanswered questions, pray and ask God to teach you how to turn these mysteries into opportunities to praise Him.

DO SOMETHING ABOUT IT

Take it a step further and say each question out loud. Then recite Paul's words in Romans 11:33, 34, and 36 as a way of letting go and worshiping God.

DAY ZERO

=FREEDOM

"Anyone who does not take his cross and follow me is not worthy of me. Whoever finds his life will lose it, and whoever loses his life for my sake will find it." **Matthew 10:38**

DAY ZERO = FREEDOM

Welcome to day Zero! Thirty days of letting go of some of the most significant things in your life and here you are. How are you doing? So far so good? I can honestly say that if you have genuinely engaged yourself in letting go of those things you have held onto for years, you are just now beginning to understand the freedom that allows you to live with a singular passion for God. I'd call this a lifestyle of worship and Zero tolerance. Worshipping the only One worthy of our lives is going to open up the world for you unlike anything you have ever experienced. There is something powerful about not needing the things of this life, because your worth is found completely in Jesus. Being able to let go, leaving the charms of the world and walking away is a big deal. That kind of freedom is so uncommon that many people will even view you as eccentric and different. Wow. Who would have ever guessed that you could be different without having to pretend to be different? Finding a life of true freedom is so rare that to live it in front of others is mesmerizing and intriguing to a lost world.

I want to introduce you to the life of Zero! The life of Zero does not fit the world's understanding of math. In fact, to the world, the math of God has never added up. Scripture says His thoughts and ways of doing things are infinitely greater than ours. To the world Zero means nothing, but as a follower of Christ it means everything. Jesus said in Matthew 10 that unless I am willing to deny myself, I am not worthy of being His follower. And if I seek to save my life (hold on) I will lose it, but if I lose it (let go) I will truly find it. All that is to say, I must become a Zero if I am going to be used by God as someone's hero. It is when I am stripped of everything and clinging to nothing that God is most glorified in me and I can be used by Him. When I have nothing to lose because I am willing to give it all for His glory, then and only then, will I experience the life that I am truly searching for.

A life of Zero is not a "poor, pitiful me" kind of life. It is not becoming everybody's religious doormat. A person who has found everything he has ever wanted, needed, or desired in Jesus is living a life of Zero. Jesus is all they need – there's nothing more to add. He is everything. It doesn't matter what they gain and it doesn't matter what they lose.

The only thing that matters is that they spend their life glorifying Him. When we recognize our total dependence on Him, God promises to clothe His followers in new and glorious garments – robes of righteousness. These are all big words describing the awesome new character that makes much of God and little of self. The Bible also warns that God will not cast His pearls before swine. This book has priceless wisdom from God's Word strung throughout the pages. What will you do with it?

Think about it like this: How many of you put on a new set of clean clothes over your dirty clothes? (If you do, you need to read a different book for serious help!) Sure, you can keep wearing the same old underwear under clean clothes but eventually it is going to catch up with you. In order for you to put on clean clothes, you have to let go of the old and start from Zero. A life of Zero gives God a blank canvas to paint His masterpiece. A Zero life is the closest you and I will ever be to the life of Jesus. Take a long, long time and allow God to do His work. Surrender everything you have been holding on to and let Him clothe you with new adventures in a new world where Jesus is everything and you are nothing… and you are OK with that!

THINK ABOUT IT

What are some areas that may not have been brought out in this book that you know need to let go of and place on the altar?

PRAY ABOUT IT

After putting your finger on a few of these, ask God to give you the strength to let go of holding on to them.

DO SOMETHING ABOUT IT

Take it a step further and make a list. Take this list to your next church worship service and go down to the altar and leave it on the altar. Then ask the pastor to pray that you would live a life where Christ is everything and you are free from the snares of this world!

ERFECT for **Wednesday nights** or **weekend retreats**!

JUSTLIKECHRIST
GET EVERYTHING YOU NEED WITH THESE BOX SETS.

∨
∨ Full of vibrant, colorful pages, these four-week studies are filled with dynamic group activities, Bible study questions, and a memory verse each week for students. Each box contains 10 student books, a DVD, and a Web license (includes your teaching lessons).

∨
∨ These pocket-sized devotional journals help students engage in God's Word day by day.

JustLikeChrist studies allow students to dig deeper in God's Word and relate the Bible to real life. Teachers and leaders access the lessons through an online delivery system.